I0488376

The Orb Series

Marjorie Sievers

Copyright © 2014 Marjorie Sievers

All rights reserved.

"…The important thing in art is signs flowing from the creative brain.
Is not the whole universe a strange skull in which meteors, suns,
comets and planets throb endlessly?"
-   Kazimir Malevich

Orb Series 1

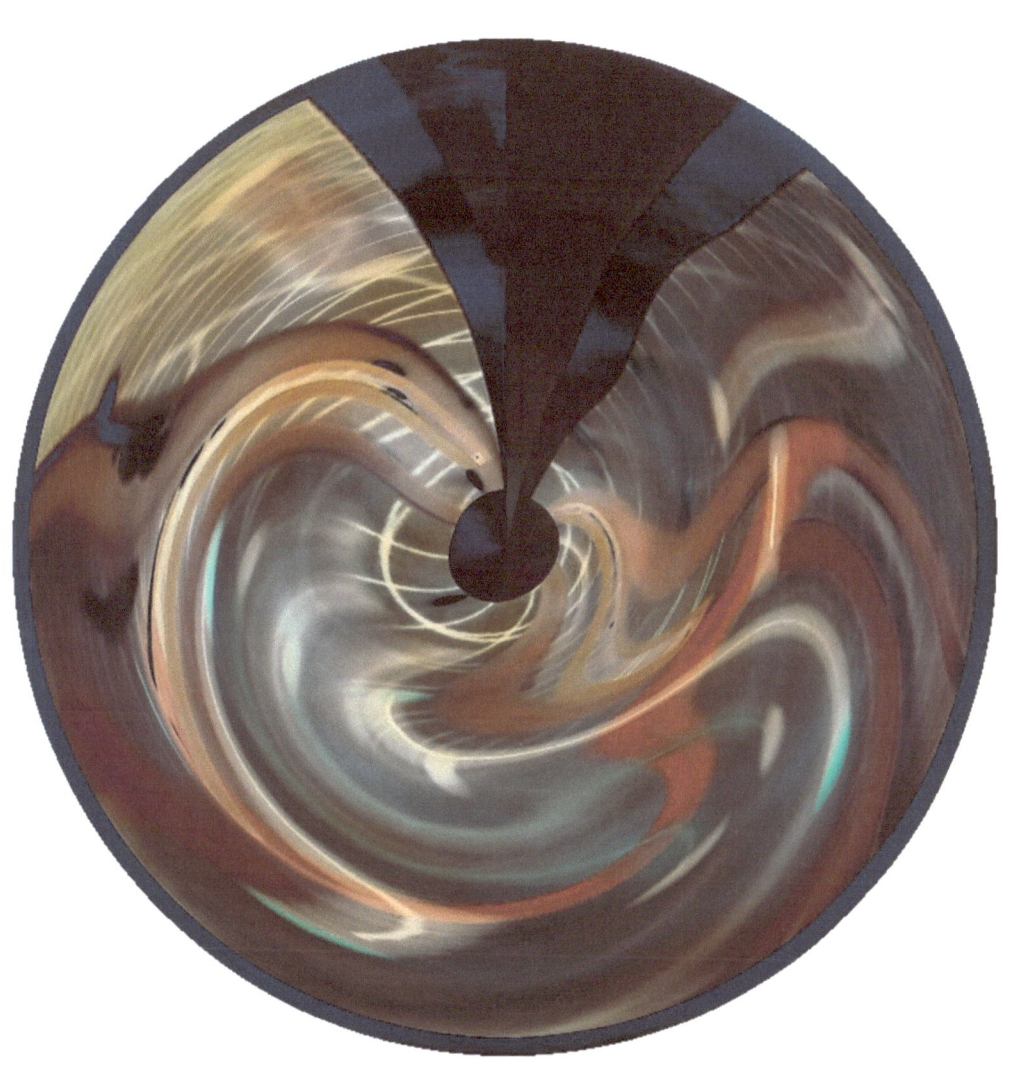

Orb Series 2

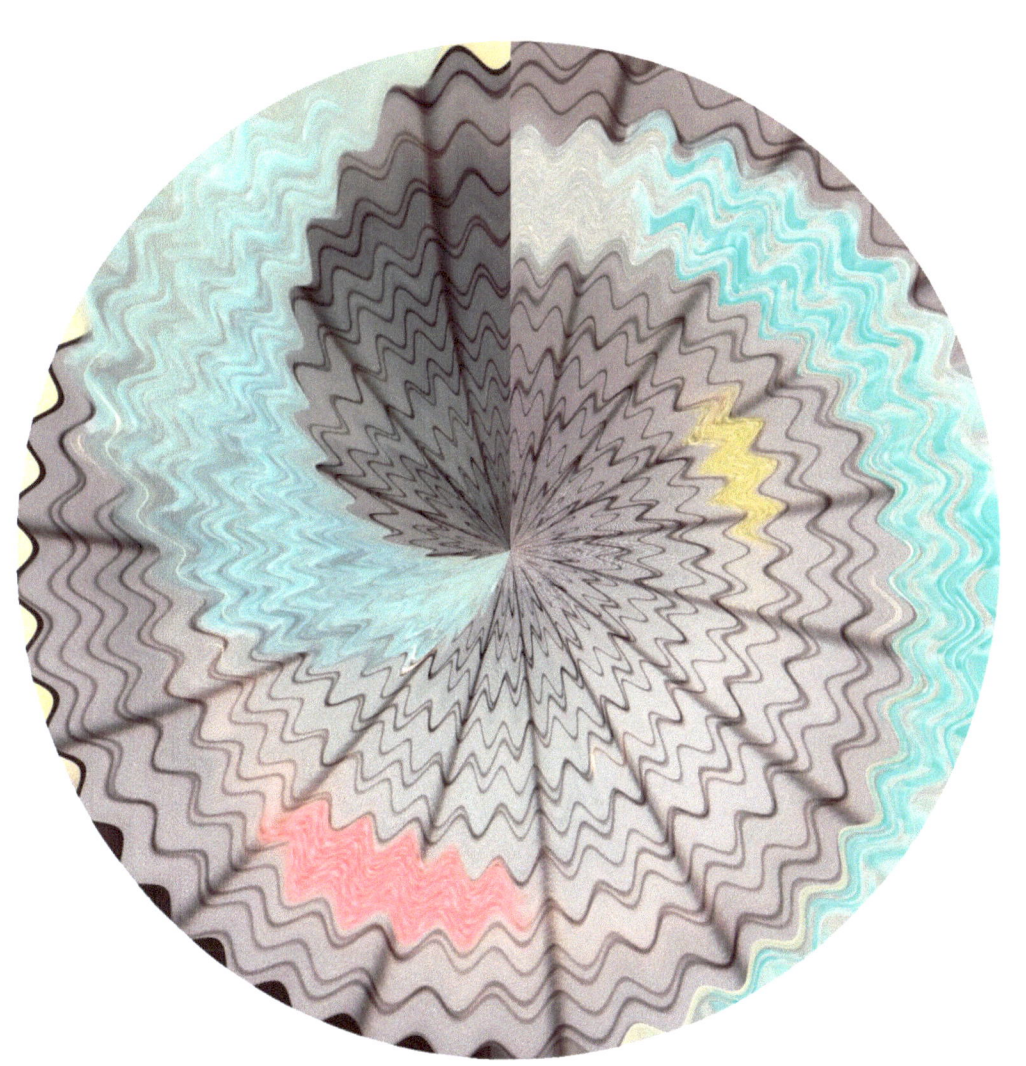

Orb Series 3

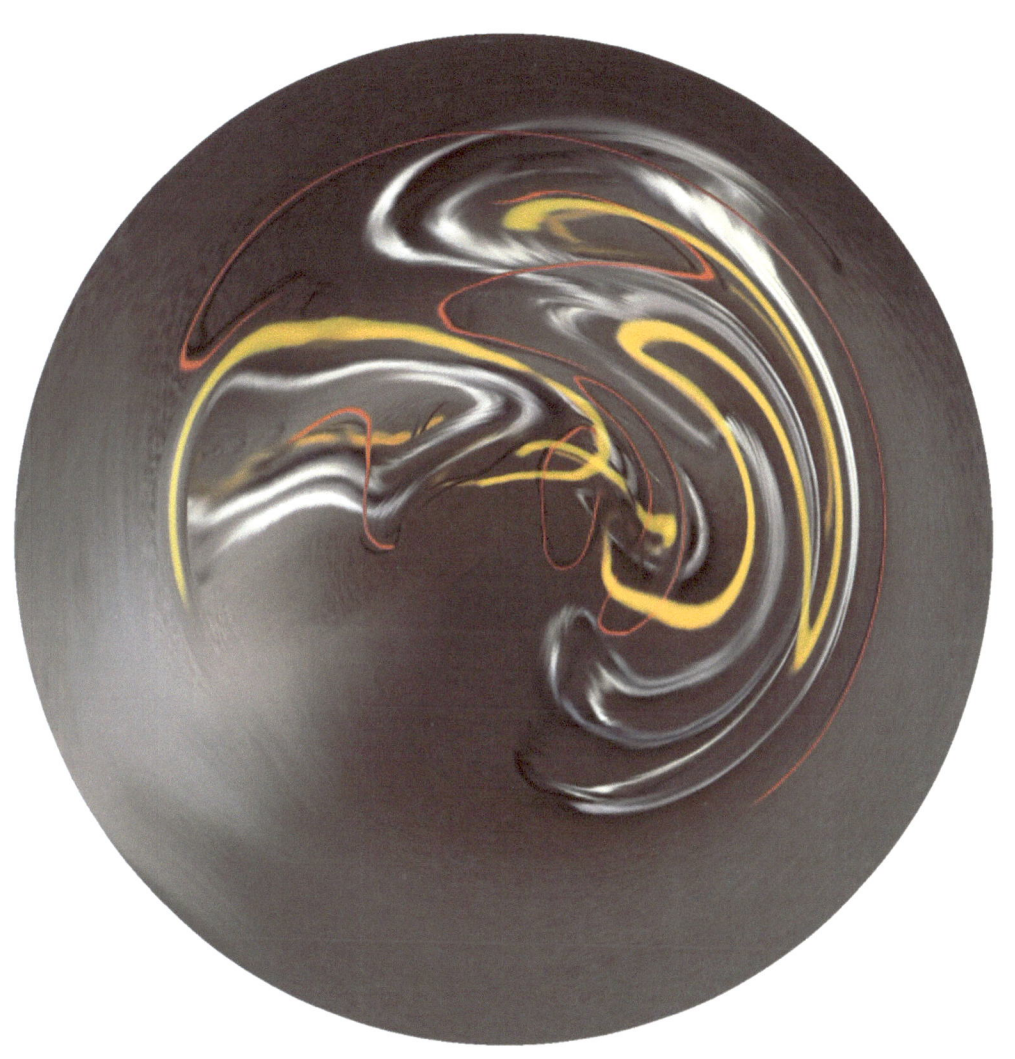

Orb Series 4

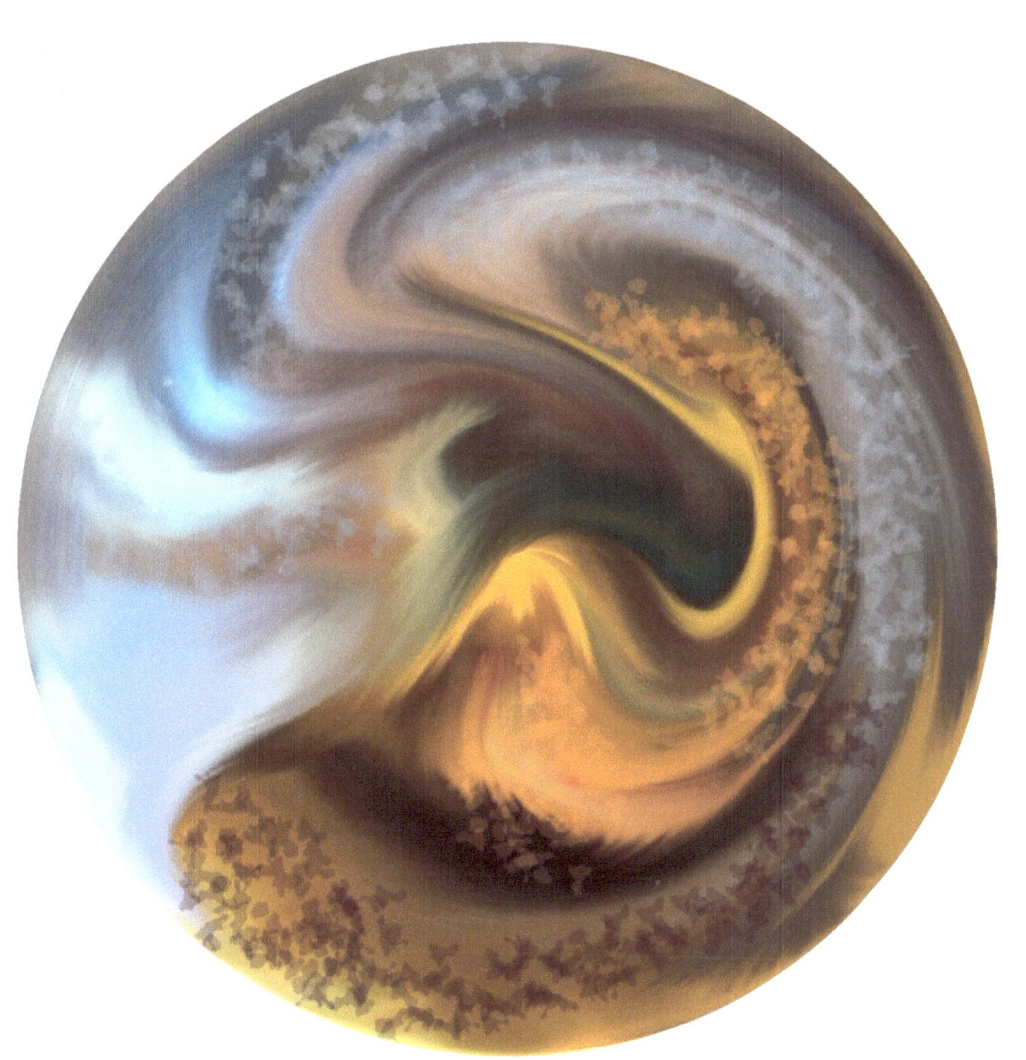

Orb Series 5

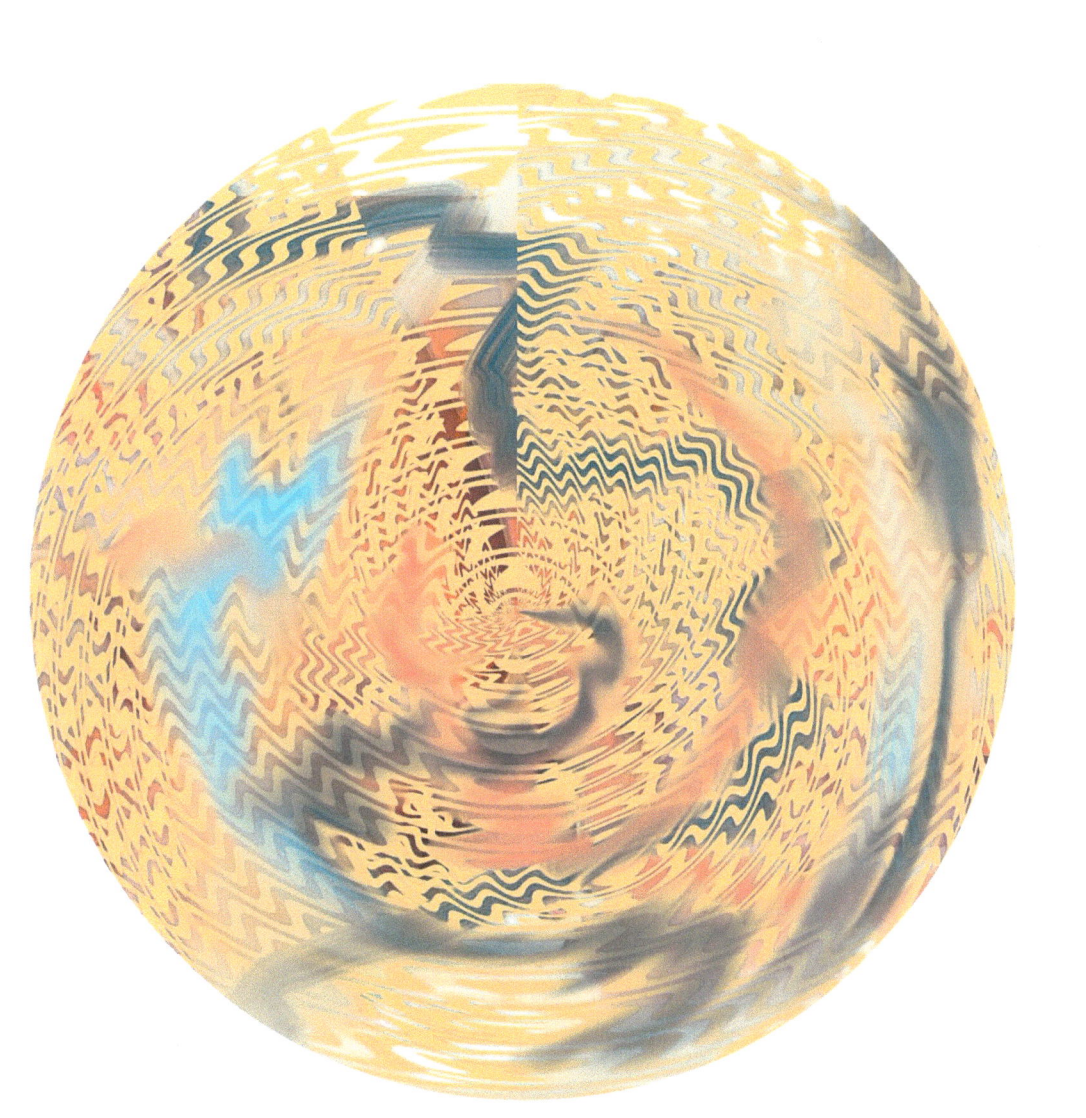

Orb Series 6

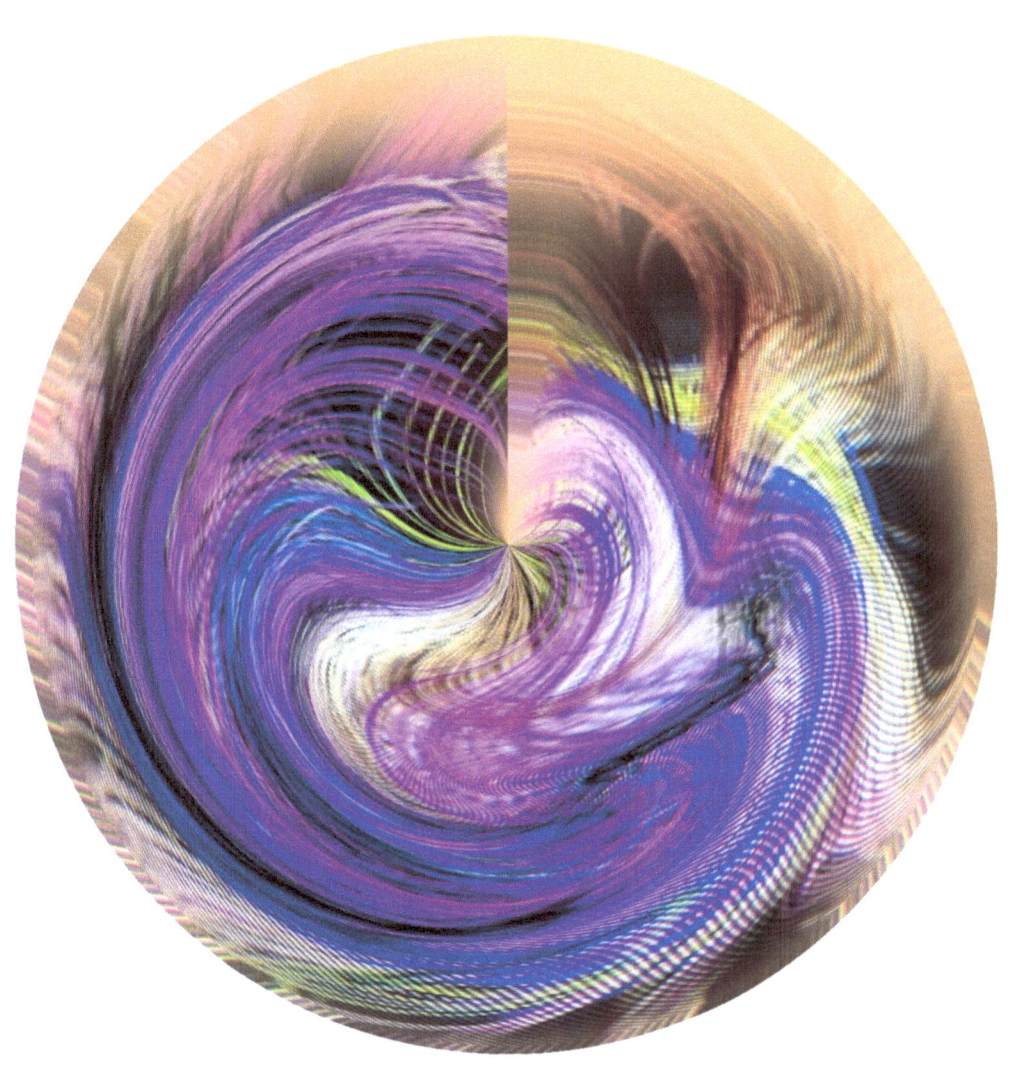

Orb Series 7

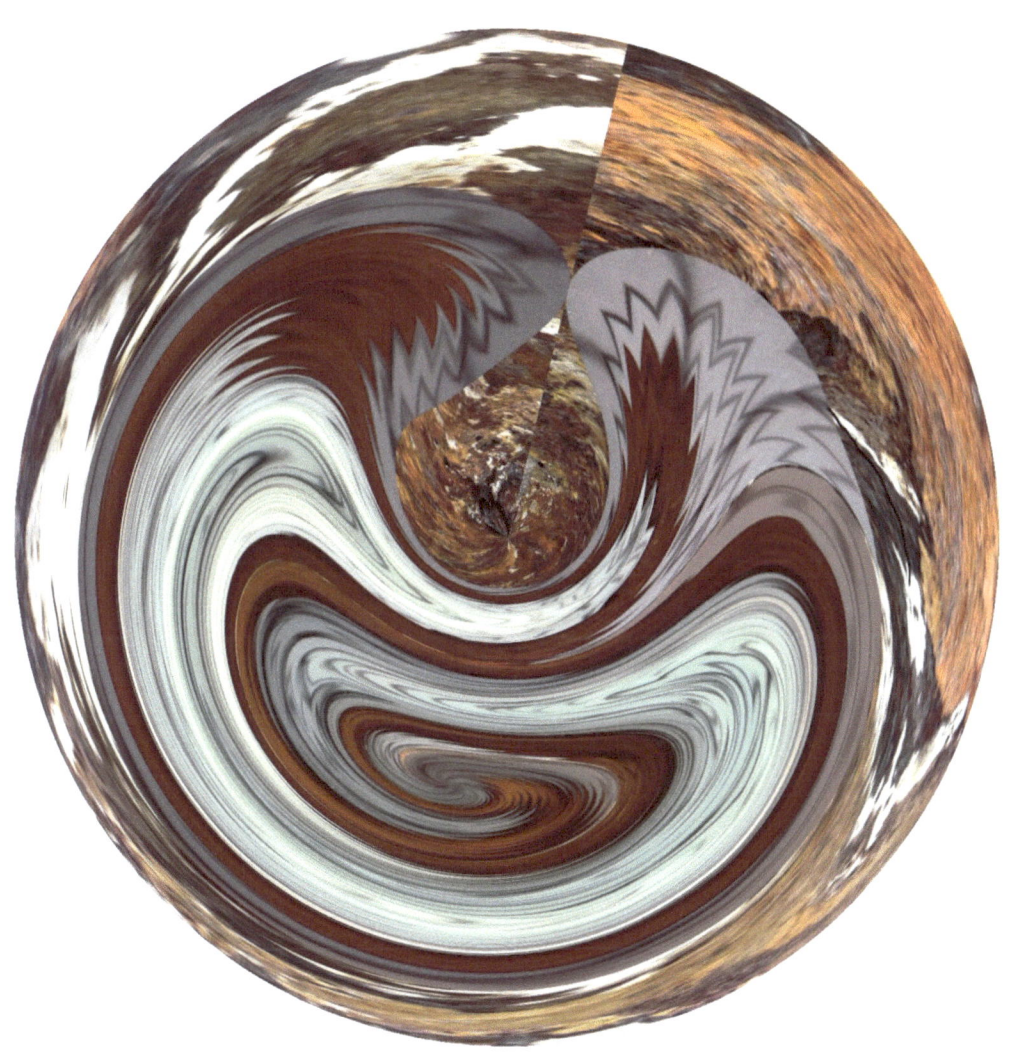

Orb Series 8

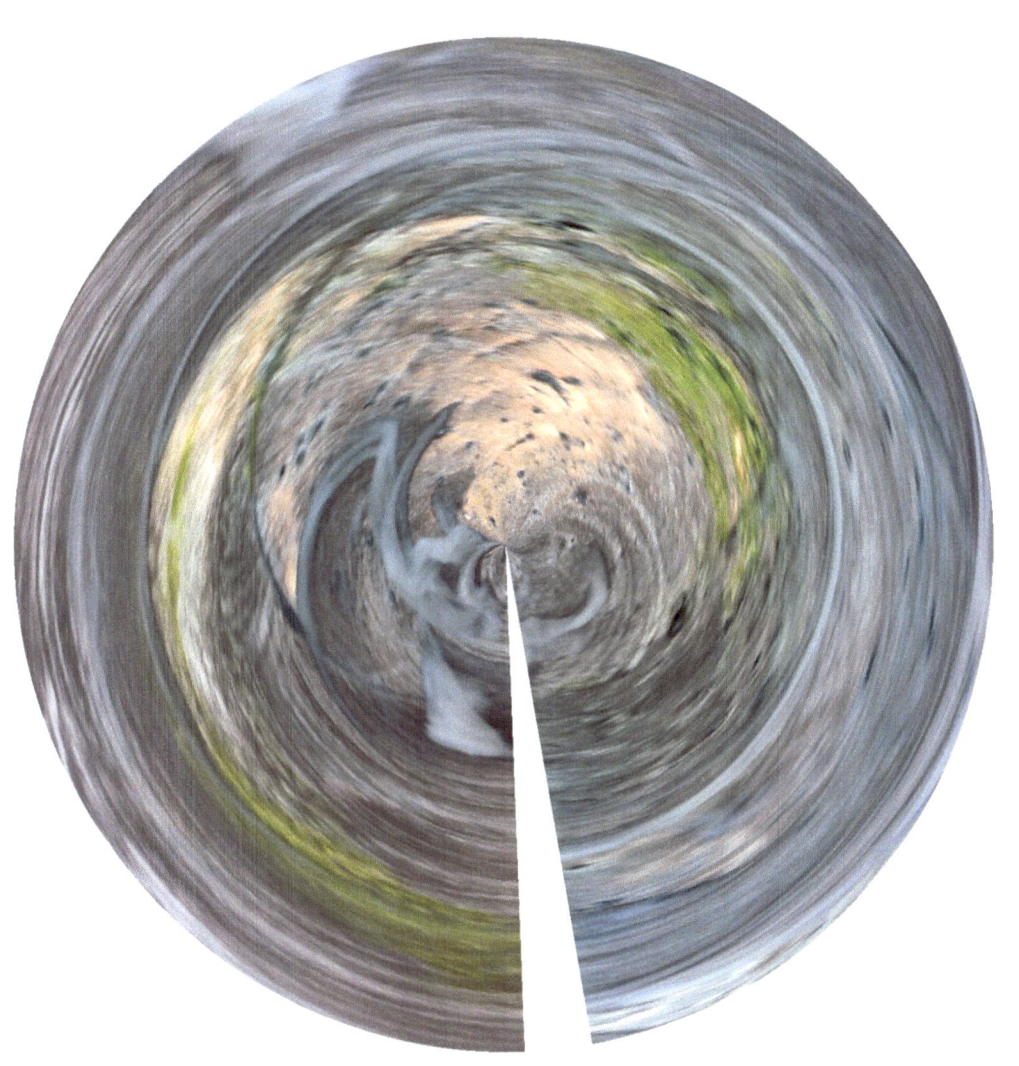

Orb Series 9

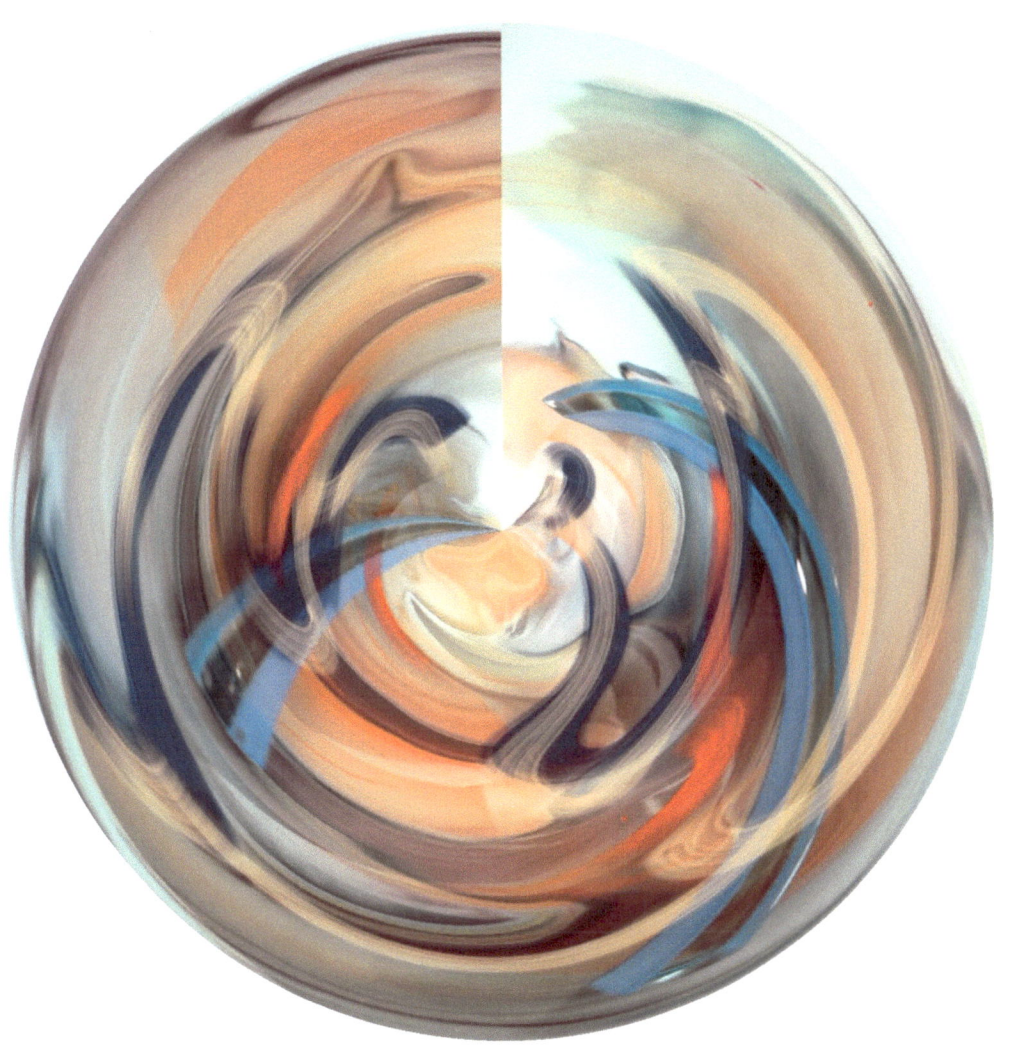

Orb Series 10

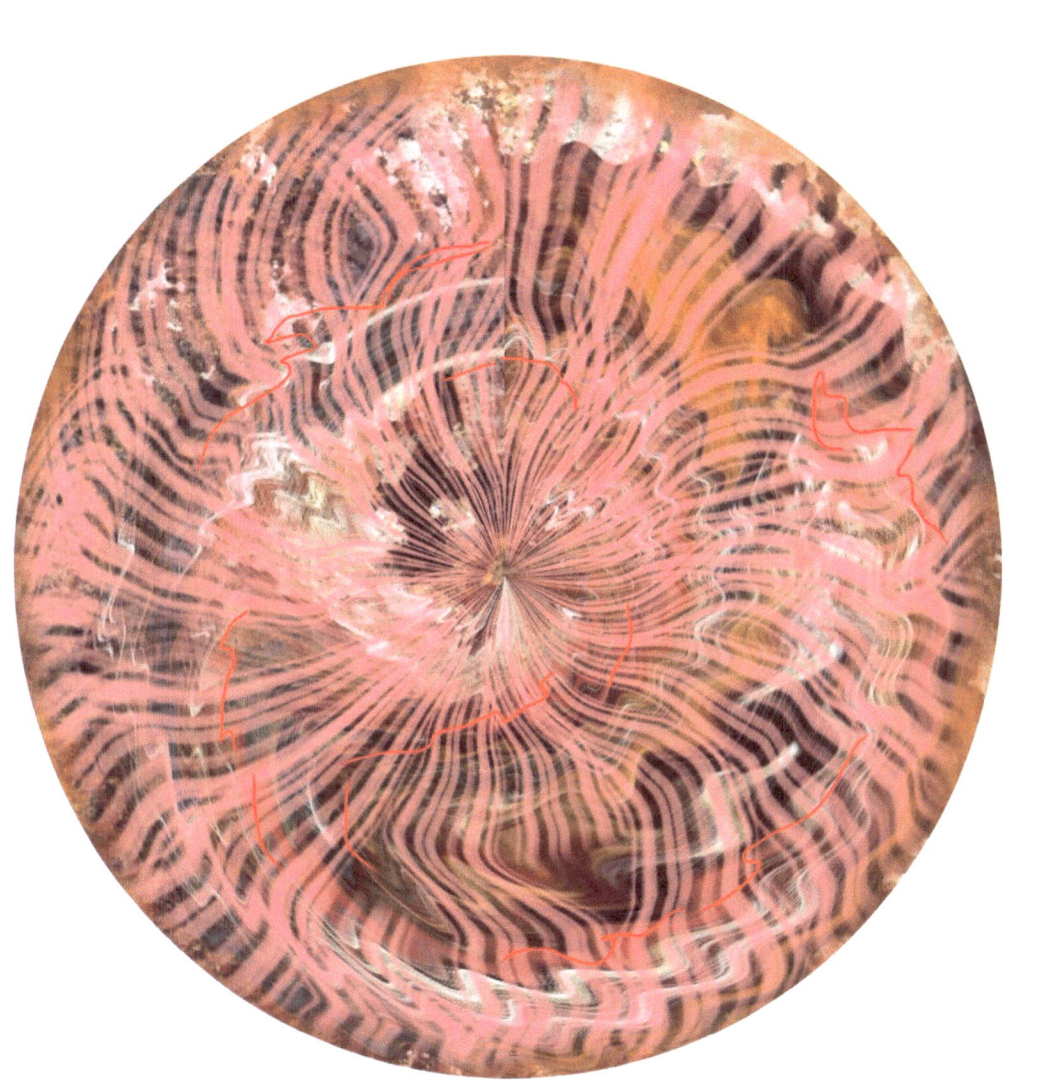

Orb Series 11

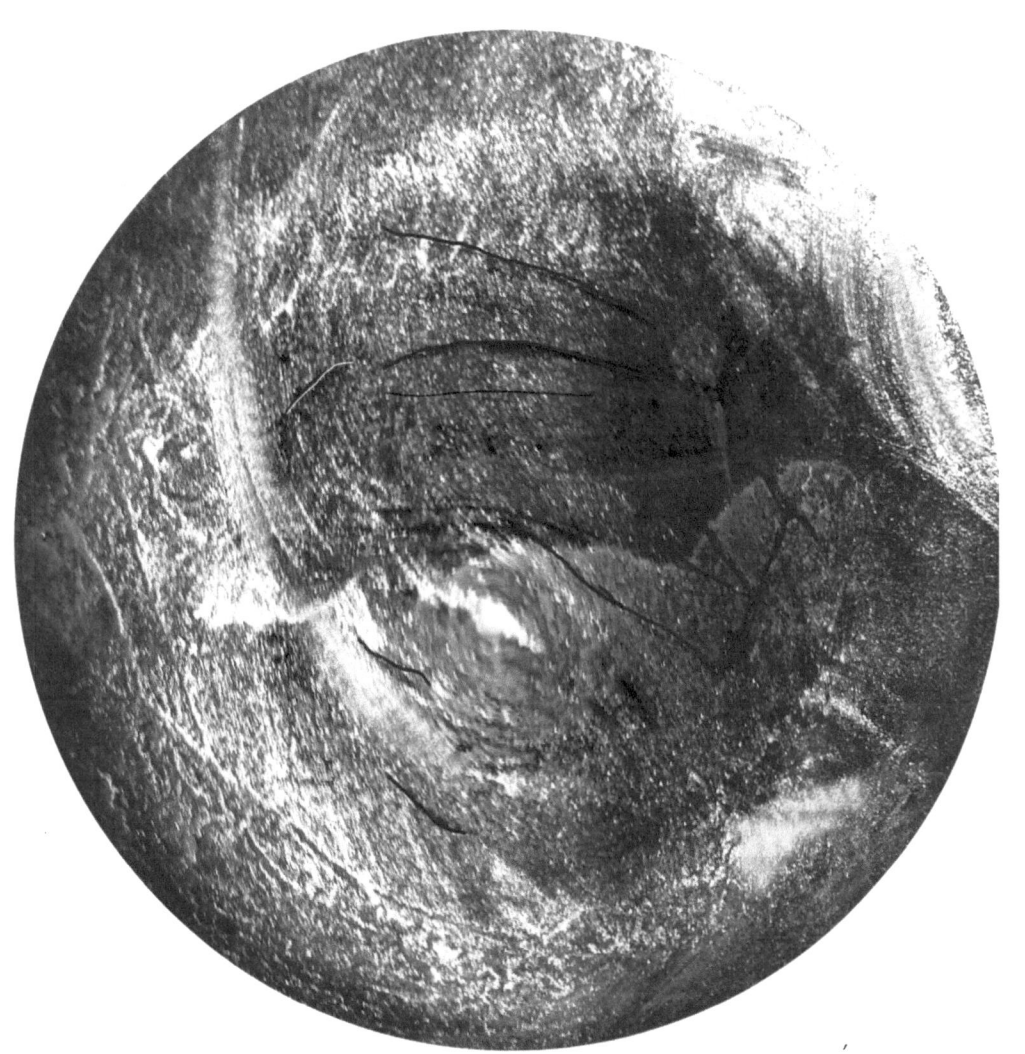

Orb Series 12

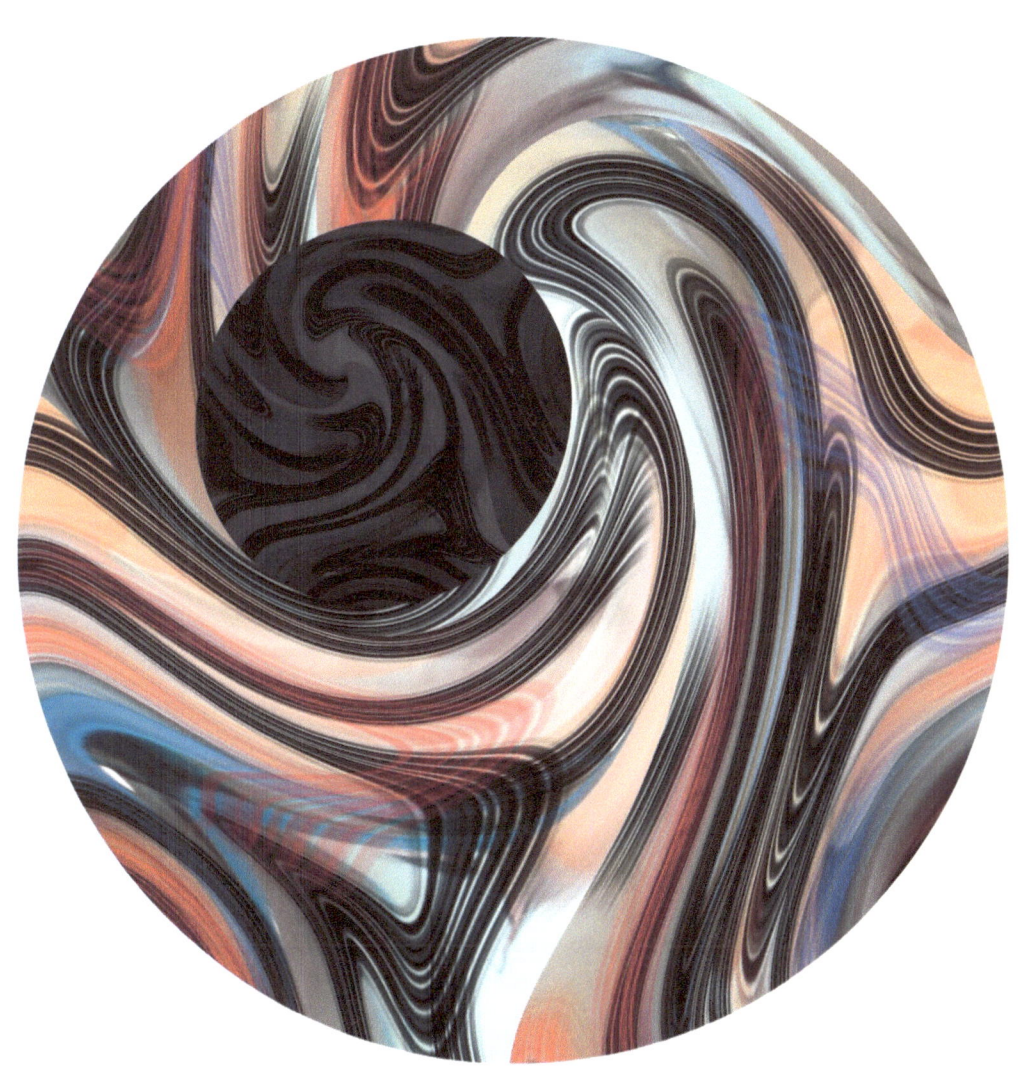

Orb Series 13

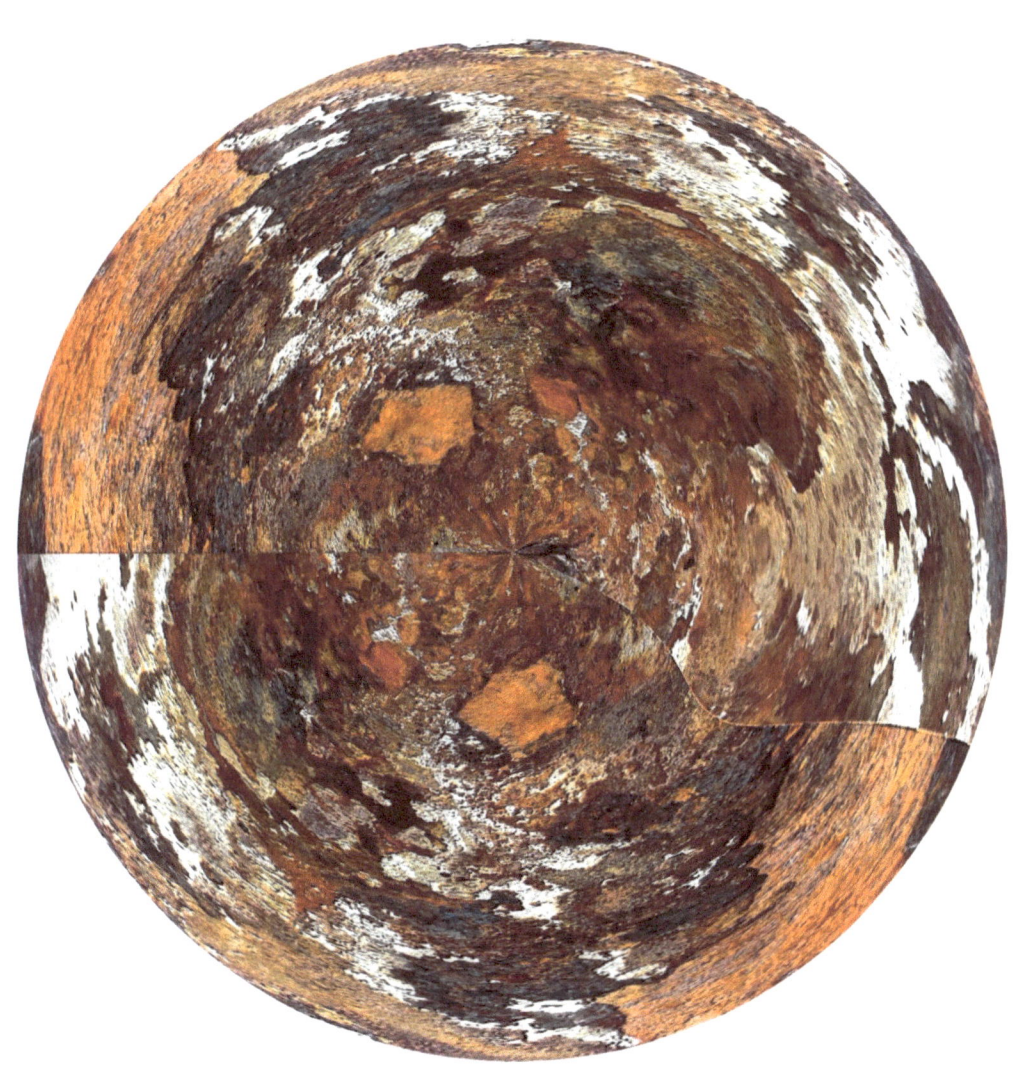

Orb Series 14

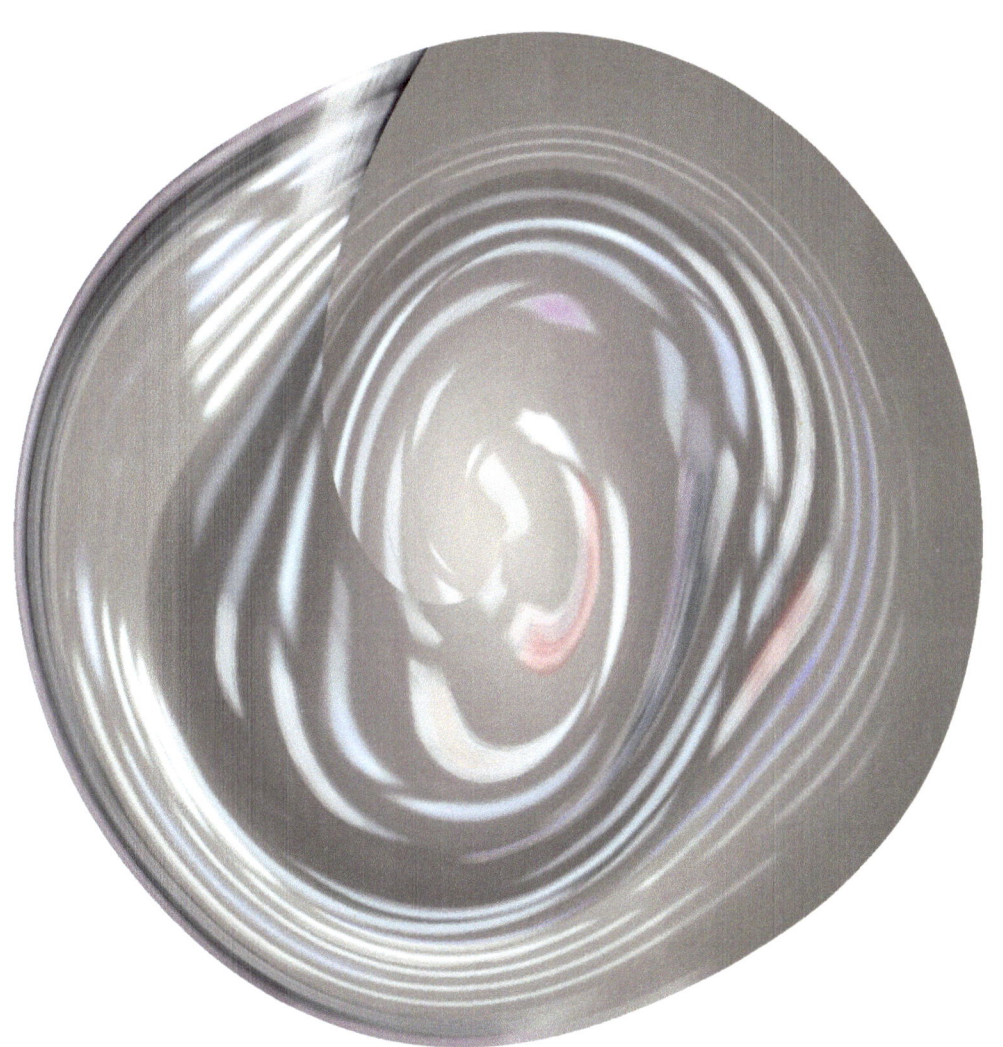

Orb Series 15

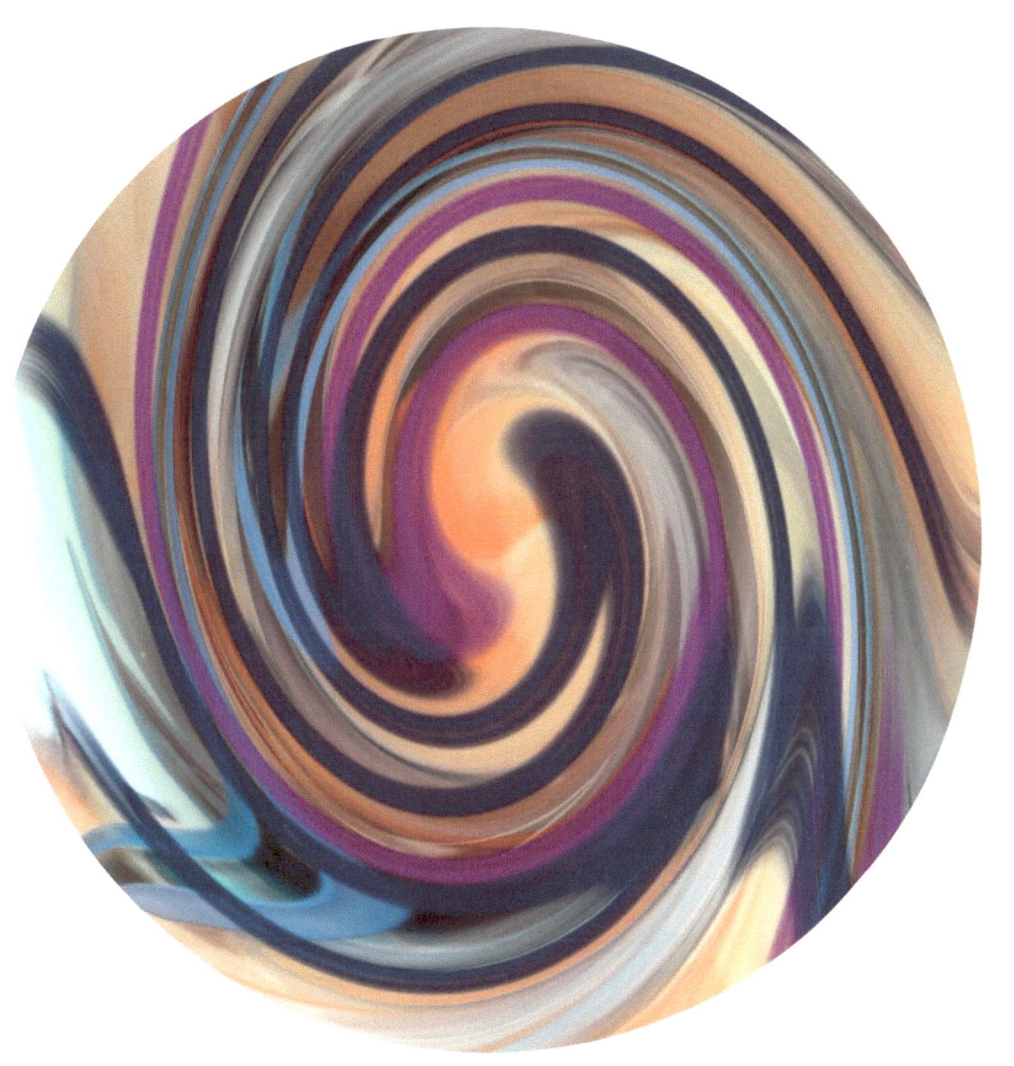

Orb Series 16

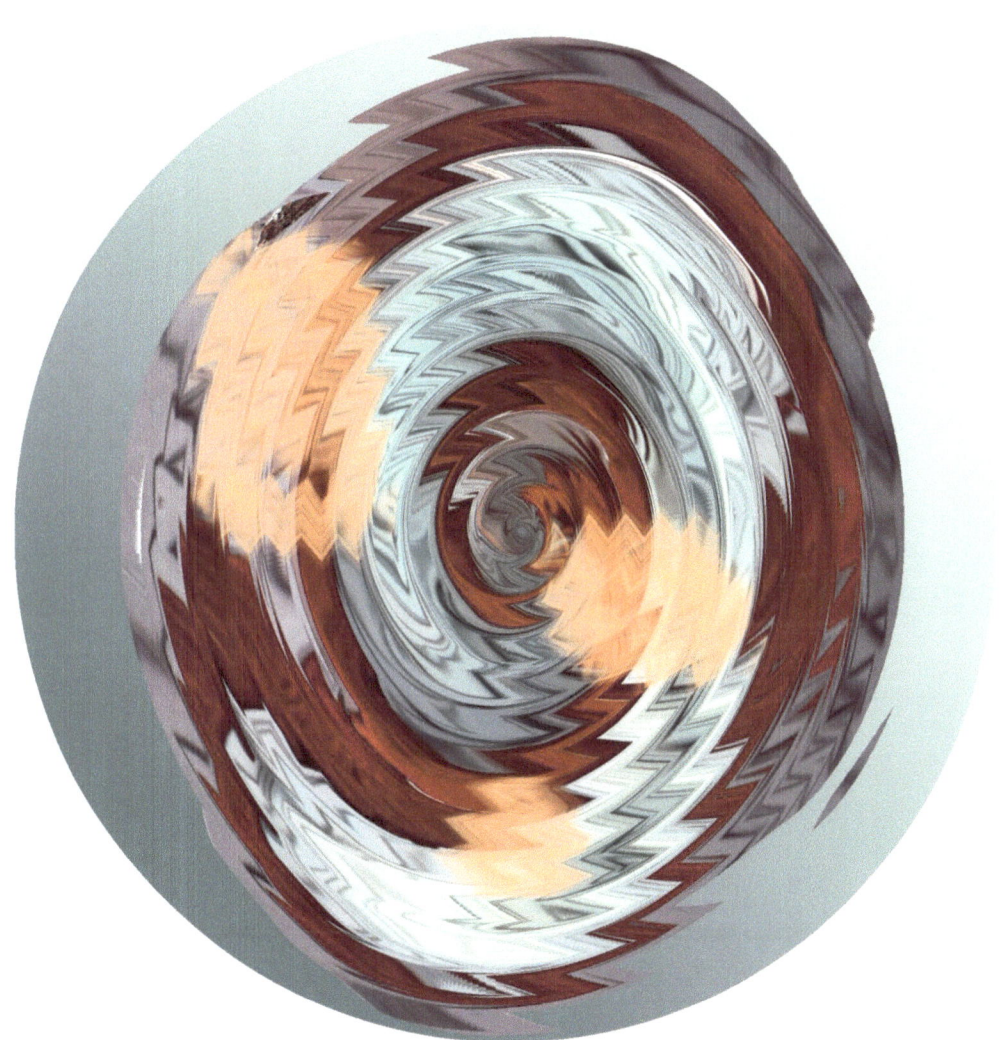

MARJORIE SIEVERS

Marjorie Sievers is a Los Angeles based artist whose works are widely exhibited. Her range of materials has included paint, metal and photography. Among her many accomplishments is the California State University Northridge Sculpture Garden, conceived and designed by her after the 1994 earthquake.

Sievers' has an MA in art from CSUN, as well as exposure to many art historical precedents including the magical landscapes of Charles Burchfield, which she saw at the Albright Knox Art Gallery when she was very young. Her wide range of non-objective images is inspired by regenerative processes, not only within our universe, but through brain impulses as well. Particularly notable is evidence that the brain can achieve a magical awareness of patterns in the atmosphere.

An inherent understanding of the connections between visionary physics and the ability of revolutionary art to evoke it underscore her interest in the micro explorations of theoretical physicists and the cosmic explorations of astrophysicists. The chaos and randomness implicit in these studies lead to the vortices of energy Sievers recreates through her art process.

Color and music have always been integral forces in her life, distinctively prevalent in her orchestration of color and in her lyrical multiplication of planes. The result is a luminous synthesis of circular fluctuation. Carl Jung stated that one of the most powerful primordial symbols was the circle. In her use of the circle, Sievers taps, not only into representations of the feminine spirit, but also into ancient and quintessential (archetypal) symbols of eternity and infinity. However, the circle represents boundaries as well. To create the illusion of circadian energies, Sievers' rhythmic momentums are confined within orbs.

Through the evocative potential of her selected medium, she is able to create intricate patterns, an illusion of the linear expansions of space. This is achieved through the thinness or thickness of lines and through the position of forms on the surface. The superimposition of one form upon the other creates added dimensions and pulsating illusions. Amorphous colors and dissonant surfaces also define space, allowing for the suggestion of celestial spheres.

Throughout her career, Sievers has employed the potential of abstraction to express cosmic ideas, namely, the spiritual realities behind corporeal form. Combining photography with images generated through an iPad program, "Orbs" is a unique and highly stylized vision of her philosophical explorations into both science and metaphysics.

Through the use of a modern medium, she attempts to reconcile the mysteries of the outer world with the forces of the inner mind. "Orbs," evokes that challenge by attempting to project ineffable primal forces through the use of color and form. When 20th century artists sought to evoke incomprehensible matters, they relied on the tactile elements of paint on canvas. Sievers' tactility stems from the use of a stylus or a brush on an iPad or on a computer touch-screen. It is a method that allows for flexibility and malleability. Further, the ability to make rapid changes produces a significant process for the evolving theories of the 21st century.

Sievers' works transcend specific meaning. As representations of inner spirits or moods of nature, she leaves their psychic effects for the viewer to decipher.

Elenore Welles

MARJORIE SIEVERS

EDUCATION

1982 California State University, Northridge Master of Arts
1980 California State University, Northridge Bachelor of Arts COMMISSIONS
2003 The Lauretta Wasserstein Earthquake Sculpture Garden. Permanent display on California State University, Northridge
1997 Arc, Eternal light and lectern for Temple Judea, Tarzana, CA
1996 Video collaboration, featuring Sergio Neglia, Ballet dancer. Mark Diamond,Choreographer. Curt Steinsor, Composer. Judith Wolf, Poet.

SELECTED EXHIBITIONS

2008 Marjorie Sievers, Solo Exhibition, Tom Wudl Studio, Los Angele, CA
2000 Five Women Painters,Claremont Graduate University, Claremont, CA
1996 Camera Transformations, Weingart Gallery, Occidental Collage, Los Angeles, CA
1991 Chaotic Harmonies, Solo Exhibition, New Image Gallery, James Madison University Harrisonberg, VA
1991 Personal References, Jose Drudis-Biada Gallery, Mount St. Mary's College, Los Angeles, CA
1982 All Media '82, Laguna Beach Museum of Art, Laguna Beach, CA

GROUP EXHIBITIONS

2011 End of An Era, Finegood Gallery, West Hills, CA
2006 Group Show, Mendenhall Sobieski Gallery, Pasadena CA
Diversity, Finegood Gallery, West Hills, CA
2005 Sculptural Forms, Lois Neiter Fine Arts, Sherman Oaks, CA
2004 Art Exhibit, Lois Neiter Fine Arts, Malibu, CA
2001 Juried exhibition, Finegood Gallery, West Hills, CA
2000 The Factory Art Show, Two person exhibition with Lois Howard
1999 Rocks no Salt, Aids Service Center, Pasadena, CA
1998 Works, Finegood Art Gallery, West Hills, CA
1996 Art Exhibit Art Exhibit, Holly Street Bar and Grill, Pasadena, CA
1991 Cycles, Southern California Women's Caucus for Art, Brand Library Art Gallery Glendale, CA. Juried.
Reaching Out, Pauline Hirsh Gallery, Los Angeles, CA, Invitational
1990 Forecast For The 90's, Los Angeles County Museum of Art Rental and Sales Gallery
1989 Concealed Forms/ Symbolic Gestures, Three person show with H. Barbara Cutler and Laurel Paley
1987 Primarily Prime, Art Source LA and Women's Caucus for Art, Juried
1986 Image Makers, Contemporary Photographers in Los Angeles, Transamerica Center Gallery, Invitational
1984 The Fourth Exhibition, Southern California Women's Caucus for Art. Juried
1982 Paradoxical Planes, Master of Arts Exhibition, California State University, Northridge.
Architectural References, Gensler and Associates, Architects, Los Angeles, CA
Invitational Alternatives, Siegfred Gallery, School of Art, Ohio University, Athens, Ohio. Traveling exhibit. Juried
1981 Los Angeles County Cultural Arts Center, Sylmar, CA. Juried
6TH Annual Cal Arts Photo Competition, Valencia, CA, Juried
1979 A Case For Art, One Person Show, California State University, Northridge.

PUBLICATIONS AND REVIEWS

2012 Book: I Touch Your Hand Across Time
2000 Catalogue: Five Women Painters Claremont Graduate University
1989 Betty Ann Brown, Concealed Forms/Symbolic Gestures. Artweek, March, 1989
1987 Catalogue: Primarily, Prime Art Source LA & Southern California Women's Caucus for Art
1984 Catalogue: The Fourth Exhibition, Southern California Women's Caucus for Art
1982 Catalogue: Alternatives, traveling exhibition, Published by the School Of Art,Ohio University, Athens, Ohio.

COLLECTIONS

Private and corporate collections through the Los Angeles County Museum of Art Rental Gallery.

www.ingramcontent.com/pod-product-compliance
Lightning Source LLC
Chambersburg PA
CBHW050358180526
45159CB00005B/2068